Rainbow Spirit

THEOLOGY

Workshop Participants
Nola J. Archie
Dennis Corowa
William Coolburra
Eddie Law
James Leftwich
George Rosendale

with
Robert Bos
Norman Habel
and
Shirley Wurst

Artwork
Jasmine Corowa

Rainbow Spirit THEOLOGY

TOWARDS AN AUSTRALIAN ABORIGINAL
THEOLOGY
BY THE RAINBOW SPIRIT ELDERS

HarperCollins*Religious*
An imprint of HarperCollins*Publishers*

HarperCollins*Religious*
An imprint of HarperCollins*Publishers* Australia

First published in Australia in 1997
Reprinted in 1997, 1999, 2000
by Dove Communications Trust
Trading as HarperCollins*Religious*
ABN 20 348 975 034
A member of HarperCollins*Publishers* (Australia) Pty Limited Group
Level 3/150 Jolimont Road, East Melbourne, Victoria 3002, Australia
http://www.harpercollinsreligious.com.au

Copyright © Wontulp-Bi-Buya 1997
Copyright © for all illustrations belongs with the artist

This book is copyright.
Apart from any fair dealing for the purposes of private study, research,
criticism or review, as permitted under the Copyright Act, no part may
be reproduced by any process without written permission.
Inquiries should be addressed to the publishers.

HarperCollins*Publishers*
Australia, New Zealand, United Kingdom, Canada and USA

National Library of Australia Cataloguing-in-Publication data:

Rainbow Spirit theology: towards an Australian Aboriginal theology.
ISBN 1 86371 703 X.
1. Aborigines, Australian – Religion. 2. Christianity – Australia.
3. Christianity and culture – Australia.
I. Rosendale, George.
270.089915

Our thanks go to those who have given us permission to reproduce copyright material in
this book. All rights of copyright holders are reserved. Particular sources of print material
are acknowledged in the text. Every effort has been made to trace the original source
material contained in this book. Where the attempt has been unsuccessful, the publishers
would be pleased to hear from the author/publisher to rectify any omission.

Unmarked Scripture quotations contained herein are translated by the authors. Scripture
quotations marked NRSV are from the New Revised Standard Version of the Bible,
copyrighted, 1989, by the Division of Christian Education of the National Council of
Churches in the United States of America, and are used by permission. All rights reserved.

Cover design: The cover painting reflects the sources and centre of the Rainbow Spirit
Theology developed in this book. The Creator Spirit is represented by the circle which
surrounds the other symbols. At the centre is the Rainbow Spirit symbol. The emu
represents Aboriginal culture; the kookaburra represents the Gospel; the sheep represents
the Bible and church traditions. Each of these symbols are located against the
background of the land. The colours used are those associated with the land.

Cover illustration by Jasmine Corowa
Printed and bound in Australia by Griffin Press on 50gsm Bulky News

9 8 7 6 5 4   00 01 02 03

Contents

PREFACE   vii

1 The Necessity of
Rainbow Spirit Theology   1

2 Doing Rainbow Spirit Theology   10

3 Land and Culture   29

4 Land and Crying   42

5 Land and Christ   55

6 Land and Reconciliation   66

APPENDICES

1 The Land and the Beginning:
Comments on Genesis 1 and 2   75

2 Abraham and the Land:
Comments on the Land
as Host Country   82

3 The Beginning and the Rainbow Spirit:
Comments on John 1   86

4 The Land in Travail, and Renewed:
Comments on Romans 8   91

5 Profiles of Aboriginal Participants   95

6 Bibliography   99

7 Acknowlegements   100

This book
is dedicated to those Aboriginal women, men
and children who gave their lives for this
land, and to those who survived
but have lost their spiritual connection
with the land

Preface

STATUS

This text is a theology in process. It represents the reflections of a group of Aboriginal leaders in Queensland who felt the need to record their thinking and circulate it for discussion among Aboriginal people, and the wider Australian church community.

This theology does not claim to be complete or comprehensive. Rather, it is a stage in a process, an invitation to other Aboriginal groups to join the dialogue and explore their Aboriginal culture as a source of mystery, meaning and theology.

Nor does the group claim to speak for any official body or group within the Australian churches. The group itself included Catholic, Anglican, Lutheran and Uniting Church members. These connections, however, were secondary: the focus of the group was its Aboriginality. The main goal was to begin to develop an indigenous theology arising from the background and experience of this group of Aboriginal Christians.

The starting point for this theology is the land as a central spiritual reality for all the participants. The writers hope that the process of reflection begun here will continue with other groups, exploring their own spiritual realities. The hope is that this text will provide a stimulus for other Aboriginal Christians to rediscover for themselves the connections between their own Aboriginal spirituality and their Christian faith.

The initial impetus for this book came from George Rosendale, who is the true elder of the group. His personal struggle to redeem his own Aboriginal culture, and discern within it profound truths which point to the Gospel, has been an inspiration to many. When George described to me his vision of an indigenous Aboriginal theology early in 1994, I was fortunate to have the support of Robert Bos, who assisted me in organising our first workshop in November of that year. All the contributors to this text say a very special thanks to George.

PROCESS

This theology is the outcome of two workshops held at Crystal Creek near Townsville, far north Queensland, in November 1994 and November 1995. The Aboriginal leaders identified with this book requested Robert Bos and myself to function as facilitators and scribes to organise and record their emerging ideas about an indigenous theology. The ideas in this book are those of the Aboriginal participants at the workshops, though the explicit wording of the text is largely mine.

During the first workshop, the beliefs, ideas and stories of the participants were recorded and formulated as statements of faith. Working from notes, Robert Bos and I then prepared a more complete draft of the text, which was circulated to all participants for comment and correction in preparation for final editing at the second workshop. At the November 1995 workshop, the text of the draft was discussed in detail. Each paragraph was read and debated; the changes to the text were recorded at the workshop. Nothing has been included in the body of the text which has not been approved by the workshop participants. Nevertheless, it must be recognised that this text represents the thinking-in-progress of the group and my wording as the editor.

At the second workshop, significant changes were made to the text prepared after the first workshop. The initial draft was tentatively called 'Kookaburra Theology', as the kookaburra was recognised as a strong symbol of good news by this Queensland group of Aboriginal people.

Between the two workshops, it became apparent to some of these Aboriginal leaders that the kookaburra was a local symbol and without parallel widespread significance throughout Australia. After considerable discussion, the Rainbow Spirit was identified as a more profound and universal symbol for an indigenous Aboriginal theology. The group was aware that this symbol might initially be rather controversial but also believed that eventually its power and significance, as well as its mystery, would give this theology greater depth and value to Aboriginal people. The introduction of the Rainbow Spirit led to a major reorientation of aspects of this indigenous theology.

The present text reflects some differences that exist between the workshop participants about the relative significance of the Rainbow Spirit. All those present at the workshop believe, however, that this is a powerful symbol, and each agreed that it was important to explore the meaning of the Rainbow Spirit stories in their respective home countries.

The artwork included in the text was also developed as part of the process of the second workshop. It reflects the working models and diagrams used by the group to help explore and develop its thinking. These models are the first phase of a possible course or teaching package we hope will be developed, based on the material in this text.

The appendices are summaries of topics developed at the first workshop, written up by the facilitators at the request of the workshop participants. They reflect an effort on the part of the two facilitators to interpret key passages of Scripture from the Aboriginal theological perspective being developed at the workshop and encapsulated in this Rainbow Spirit Theology.

ACKNOWLEDGMENTS

We acknowledge the financial support of several bodies in the development and publication of this book:

- the University of South Australia for research funds to cover the costs of the initial workshop, held in November 1994;
- World Vision for funds to cover the costs of the second workshop, held in November 1995;
- Wontulp Bi Buya for facilitating the distribution of these funds and supporting the project;
- the Charles Strong Trust for funds to assist with the editing and publishing of the manuscript.

PARTICIPANTS

The core group of Aboriginal leaders at the first workshop were Pastor William Coolburra, Rev. Dennis Corowa, Rev. Eddie Law, Rev. James Leftwich and Rev. George Rosendale. These leaders were joined by Elder Nola J. Archie for the second workshop. The artist, Miss Jasmine Corowa, joined the group during the second workshop. A thumbnail sketch of these Aboriginal participants is included in the appendices.

The facilitators, Robert Bos and I, were assisted by

Shirley Wurst, who functioned as scribe at both workshops to ensure that all the ideas were preserved and all the changes recorded.

Norman Habel
Facilitator

NOTE ON TERMINOLOGY

There was considerable discussion at both workshops about the use of the terms 'Dreaming', 'Dreamtime' and 'totem'. Members of the group had quite different understandings of the meaning and the appropriateness of these terms. We were aware that the term 'Dreamtime' probably arose from Spencer and Gillan's use of the Aranda word *Alcheringa*. The term 'the Dreaming' is an alternative term used by other scholars to express the same concept. The term 'totem' is also a complex concept, derived from studies focusing on the Native American peoples.

The problem for us is that these terms have been appropriated and used in different ways by Aboriginal people in Queensland, let alone people in the rest of Australia.

Some members of our group, like many Aboriginal Australians, are not happy with the term 'the Dreaming' because in the English language it seems to refer to something vague and dreamlike, something that is not real. The Aboriginal concept that the term 'the Dreaming' attempts to convey refers to an essential part of reality, a spiritual dimension of reality that has existed from the beginning.

We avoided the term 'Dreamtime' because it suggests that this reality only existed at the time of creation; we Aboriginal people know that this reality continues to exist in the present. Furthermore, to refer to our creation stories as 'Dreamtime stories' is to suggest to many English speakers that they are not true stories, that they are fairy stories.

In spite of these difficulties, we sometimes use the term 'Dreaming' as a word to convey that powerful spiritual reality which was active in the creation time, in the beginning, and continues as a reality that gives spiritual life to our present reality.

Some members of our group spoke of 'my Dreaming' when referring to the story and symbol of their identity as individuals within the Aboriginal world. Other workshop participants used the expression 'my totem' to express the same reality. At other times, some of us used the term 'my story' as the most appropriate way of expressing all these aspects of our world.

chapter one

THE NECESSITY OF RAINBOW SPIRIT THEOLOGY

High on the branch of a kauri pine in a Queensland rainforest, a small bird rests. Having previously fed on the sweet fruit of the Ficus, the bird excretes seeds and leaves them in a small, wet patch of manure on the branch, then flies away.

Several weeks later, in the humid conditions, one fertilised seed has sprouted many leaves. Long, hair-like roots have begun to snake downwards, seeking soil and moisture. The seed has come back to the land to grow and develop. Having reached the humus-rich floor of the rainforest, the parasitic fig draws aloft life-giving nutrients.

In the months that follow, the young tree flourishes. High in the canopy, a trunk and branches are formed. Meanwhile, the thin hair-like roots begin to embrace its host and thicken.

In time, the roots of the fig swell so much that the generous host is slowly crushed. The parasitic plant is commonly known as the strangler fig.

Late last century, missionaries came to Aboriginal groups in North Queensland. These well-meaning men and women themselves suffered dangers, hardship and isolation. In time, they established permanent settlements, medical clinics, farms and churches.

Being convinced of the vital importance of the Christian message, they sought to convert our people to their Christian beliefs and habits. Some tried to understand the customs of our people. One or two tried to understand our religion. For the most part, our religious beliefs and ceremonies were regarded as pagan, barbaric and evil. The sooner these were replaced with civilised Christianity, the better for all concerned; or so they thought!

Because most missionaries had little regard for the beliefs and practices which were central to the way of life of our people, and actively promoted a European culture as superior, our people became confused. During the workshop, one of the participants remembered how 'white German missionaries brought us a white German Jesus... Now I can finally see that Jesus Christ is like me. He has my skin, my colour — everything like me. Now I know Christ camped among us, built his humpy among ours'.

Many of our people were humiliated by punishments handed out by the foreigners. The rule of the missionaries was supported by the power of the government — and its police force. Our elders had a sacred responsibility as the caretakers of this land and its resources. Because they could no longer exercise this care, they lost their purpose in life. The core beliefs of our people were rejected. The self-esteem of our people was destroyed. And the spirit of our people was crushed.

Many Aboriginal people today affirm the positive message of the Gospel brought by the missionaries, but see the rejection of our traditional culture as unnecessary and destructive. The Christian message was imposed from above and, like the strangler fig in the story, gradually choked the life out of our rich spiritual tradition — and therefore out of our people themselves. How much better it would have been for our people if that message had been planted in Australian soil, and encouraged to take on its own form and find its own place in its new cultural environment.

Now that many dozens of Christian Aboriginal people

have undertaken formal theological education, we have begun to evaluate the theology and history of the missions in the light of our own reading of the Scriptures and our own experience as Christian Aboriginal people. This book represents one such evaluation.

To help our people face the future with confidence, we need to examine closely what remains of our traditional spirituality in the light of the Christian Gospel. We have begun to construct our own Christian theology to strengthen our people for the future and to offer new directions for Australia. This book represents one step in that direction. It represents a new expression of pride in our culture and in our faith.

As one participant at the workshop confessed:

> Jesus was thrust down my throat. I was not encouraged to think for myself or allow a theology to grow from within me as an Aboriginal. I had to get rid of the 'dependency baggage'. I was told what to do, what to think, where to live. I was not free. I now need to think things through, to feel my own needs, work through my own faith, and develop my own Aboriginal theology.

This task is not an exercise in intellectual game-playing. It is literally a matter of life and death. Behind the tragedy of many Aboriginal communities (poor health, high infant mortality, low life-expectancy, high unemployment, poor housing, alcoholism, malnutrition, deaths in custody — the list goes on) lies a deep spiritual crisis.

Because of the approach of many missionaries and the attitude of non-indigenous Australians in general, many of our people feel a deep sense of shame, a lack of worth and a feeling of being lost.

Our people have been entrusted by the Creator Spirit with the care of the land and the associated ceremonies. In most parts of Australia, they are unable to care for their land and ensure its continued fruitfulness because it has been taken over by the immigrants. The ceremonies have lost much of their meaning for most Aboriginal people. The spiritual line of succession, from the time of creation through countless generations, has now been broken. And deep inside, our people live with guilt and hopelessness.

In spite of the massacres, the poisonings, the epidemics, the tearing apart of families and all the other horrendous sufferings of our people, we have survived.

Our task now is to mould a new spirituality that will bring healing to our people, that will create a sense of pride and identity in our youth and strengthen them to take their rightful place both in this nation and in the world community. This book affirms our past spirituality as the work of the Creator Spirit and provides a basis for a bold indigenous faith.

This book is important for a second reason. In some churches, the old Christian colonialism continues. Pastors and priests continue to impose on our people a European expression of the Christian message as though this were the only valid expression of the truth. Most of our Aboriginal pastors have been indoctrinated into this European Christianity. And the very things which crushed the spirit of our people in the past continue to do so today.

Many of our people suffer silently inside, but they are too polite or confused to declare their suffering openly.

Because we respect our European and Western Christian leaders, we want to help them come to a fresh understanding of Christianity which is faithful to the Scriptures — and is also genuine Good News for all people. It is our hope that these Christian leaders will be able to see the damage they are doing and free themselves from the European cultural bondage in which their theology is imprisoned.

Thirdly, we believe that Rainbow Spirit Theology has something to offer the whole of Australia. In our country, too, economic values often take precedence over human and spiritual values. Genuine cooperation — in which all parties are respected and everyone wins — is replaced by confrontation and competition. The wholesale destruction of our land continues. In the sixty or more thousand years that our people have been in this continent, we have learned to live in this land. We want to share it with all Australians in a way that will ensure a better future for all our children.

The Spirit of God is speaking to and through Aboriginal Australians. God does not speak to us first and foremost through European and Western theology. God accepts us as we are. Our people need to be free of the terrible burden of believing that they need to think and live like Europeans before they can be Christians.

We need to chop down the strangler figs which are choking us so that we can be free to be what God wants us to be. We need to hear the Gospel expressed in our own language and culture. Only then will the spirits of our people be free. Then we will all, Aboriginal and immigrant, join in the joyous laughter of the kookaburra, and we will all, Aboriginal and immigrant, recognise the rainbow as a symbol of our spiritual unity in Christ.

One of the workshop participants summarised our task in these words:

> The Jewish people struggled to lift the temple veil that shrouded God as revealed to us in Jesus Christ. We are in the process of lifting the veil of God's revelation in our culture. We are lifting the veil to see God, to see Christ in ourselves and our culture. In so doing, we are connecting with peoples in every culture. For Aboriginal people, Christ was behind a curtain. Some were able to see Christ through a small gap in that curtain. We now need the courage to push our heads through the curtain so that we really can see God in Christ, in our own culture, in our own world, where we are.

We also recognise that during the history of the Christian church in Australia, there have been missionaries and other church people who, in spite of government policies and the paternalistic attitude of most churches, have supported Aboriginal people. Some supporters helped us keep our land, some opposed oppressive policies and some intervened, risking their lives to save Aboriginal people from being killed. In more recent times, some supporters have genuinely helped us in our struggle for justice and the preservation of our culture. Sad to say, these supporters in the church have been all too few.

The Sources of our Rainbow Spirit Theology

chapter two

DOING RAINBOW SPIRIT THEOLOGY

1. Doing Rainbow Spirit Theology is not new. In recent years, Christian Aboriginal people have been reflecting openly about the links between Christian teachings and their Aboriginal culture.

When the European missionaries first arrived, we Aboriginal people found it difficult to accept the claim of many missionaries that all or most of our Aboriginal culture was wrong. In more recent times, Christian Aboriginal people have come to realise that much of what we learned from the Scriptures, especially the Old Testament, is similar to what we knew from our own culture.

Christian Aboriginal thinkers have reflected on these similarities and made many connections between our own Aboriginal culture and our Christian faith. This reflection, whether written or oral, is a living and developing indigenous Aboriginal theology.

We have called the indigenous theology developed by our group 'Rainbow Spirit Theology'. This theology endorses the writings of our leaders such as Djiniyini Gondarra, who wrote the following in the introduction to his series of reflections on Aboriginal theology, *Let My People Go*:

> During the past ten years there have been many Christian Aborigines, both men and women, who have gained a deeper understanding about God. In this way they have realised the great contribution our culture can make towards a deeper understanding of the Christian faith in Australia today. (1986, p. iv)

2. Rainbow Spirit Theology assumes that God the Creator Spirit has been speaking through Aboriginal culture from the beginning.

European missionaries were mistaken when they claimed that they had been sent to reveal God to spiritually blind Aboriginal Australians. God, the Creator Spirit, was already here. Our Aboriginal culture was already spiritual, more overtly spiritual than the European culture of those who invaded Australia. God was already speaking to us through the law revealed in the land.

The New Testament Letter to the Hebrews talks of

God speaking in many and various ways to our ancestors (Hebrews 1:1). We believe that this text applies equally well to the ancestors of our Aboriginal people as it does to the ancestors of the people of Israel. The Creator Spirit spoke to us in many ways, especially through the land which links us to the Creator Spirit.

As one of our workshop group said:

> Aboriginal culture is spiritual. I am spiritual. Inside of me is spirit and land, both given to me by the Creator Spirit. There is a piece of land in me, and it keeps drawing me back like a magnet to the land from which I came. Because the land, too, is spiritual.
>
> This land owns me. The only piece of land I can claim a spiritual connection with — a connection between me and the land — is the piece of land under the tree where I was born, the place where my mother buried my afterbirth and umbilical cord. The spiritual link with that piece of land goes back to the ancestors in the Dreaming. This is both a personal and sacred connection — between me and the land, me and my ancestors.

In his study guide for Nungalinya College called *Spirituality for Aboriginal Christians*, George Rosendale writes:

> Long before Christianity came here, our people had faith in Yiirmbal as their God. They believed that their creator would provide for them, they believed if they got sick he would save them. He

would look after them and he would care for them. They had faith to know that Yiirmbal would do all these things for them. (1993, p. 3)

It is important to realise that we Aboriginal people have different names for God (see chapter 3, point 3).

3. The Rainbow Spirit has been chosen as the symbol for this theology because the Rainbow Spirit represents life and rebirth.

Rainbow Spirit Theology reflects a hope of rebirth among Christian Aboriginal people that links us to the powerful symbols, stories and truths of our culture. One of our most powerful symbols is the Rainbow Spirit.

As the Creator, the Rainbow Spirit is often portrayed by our Aboriginal artists as a powerful snake who emerged from the land, travelled the landscape leaving trails of life, and then returned to the land through caves, waterholes and other sacred sites.

Early Christian missionaries associated this snake image with Satan and the story of the Fall in Genesis 3. They saw the snake as a pagan symbol of fertility religion and condemned it as evil. They did not understand the profound significance of the Rainbow Spirit for our people. For a long time, Christian Aboriginal people have accepted the teaching of the missionaries that the Rainbow Spirit is a symbol of evil.

We believe it is time to return to this symbol in our culture to help us rediscover our spiritual identity as

Christian Aboriginal people.

We believe that the Rainbow Spirit is not the source of evil but of life. In our culture, the Rainbow Spirit was sometimes portrayed and experienced as powerful and frightening, like the God of the Old Testament at Mt Sinai (Exodus 19:16–19, 21). But that image reflects the mystery and majesty which now is to be respected but no longer feared.

As the Creator, the Rainbow Spirit gave life to all our ancestors and all the creatures — the trees, plants, animals and birds — and to the landscape itself. The Rainbow Spirit is the symbol of the new day which dawns after the rain sent by the Rainbow Spirit. The rainbow that appears in the sky is the peace after the storm, the promise of God to care for all creation (Genesis 9). The Rainbow Spirit is also the guardian of the law, the land and the sacred places in the land.

The Rainbow Spirit is an important being in our ancient stories of the beginning. In these stories, the Rainbow Spirit swallowed young people and regurgitated them as young adults. Within the Rainbow Spirit, these young people were being reborn, transformed into new beings. They died to youth and rose as adults. This story, in many forms, was relived by young people in their initiation ceremonies.

In this theology, we seek to redeem this profound symbol and fill it with new meaning in the light of the Gospel (see chapter 5). For us, the Rainbow Spirit is a symbol of the ancient mystery of our culture and the promise of a new beginning.

4. Rainbow Spirit Theology functions with the model of four directions in the land, using the Aboriginal custom of orienting to the movement of the sun. Three streams come together, providing the sources for doing this theology. A fourth stream flows from this theology into the future.

Theology is a way of organising our thinking about God. Theology is making sense of God according to a model. The model that helps us do our theology is that of the four directions in the land. The forces creating our theology come to us from three directions, and flow in a new direction for the future.

The South represents truths from within, insights derived from our Aboriginal culture. The North represents the wisdom of ancient sources from the past. The East is the Gospel, and the direction which gives us our bearings. The West represents strength for our people in the future.

The model for this theology is outlined in the following diagram:

5. The stream from the South represents truths from our culture, and the violation of the culture. We discover these truths in our land, our stories, our teachings, our history and our ceremonies. The inspiration for discovering these truths comes from the Rainbow Spirit at the centre of our Aboriginal culture.

Since we believe that the Creator Spirit has been present, giving life and meaning to our culture from the beginning, we can turn to our understanding and experience of our culture as a key source for our theology. Insights which reveal the presence of the Creator Spirit among our people are valuable contributions to our indigenous theology. We are like the householder in Jesus' parable who brings out treasure old and new (Matthew 13:52). Some of these treasures, as Jesus says through this parable, have been hidden since the foundation of the world. As we search our ancient sources, we hope to bring out these treasures to enrich our theology, and teach them to our children.

The experience of this same Spirit, who has been with us during 200 years of suffering under the oppression of alien cultures, is also valuable. Christian Aboriginal people in Australia can indeed identify closely with the suffering of Christ.

The symbol of the South is the emu, a bird who tracks the land and who searches with intense curiosity. Other Aboriginal groups have different symbols; it depends on their stories of the beginning, their Dreaming stories. Our goal is to search our experience and culture to discover

the tracks of God, the Creator Spirit, in our past and our present. Like Aboriginal people, the emus maintain strong kinship ties. And like the emu, many of our people have learned to track even the faintest trails through the land. In this theology, we are tracking the trail of the Creator Spirit through our culture.

As Djiniyini Gondarra writes:

> The Reformation gave Western culture the freedom to explore that dialogue [between faith and culture] in many directions. The Western church has not, in turn, given that same freedom to Aboriginal people to explore that dialogue through their own culture. We now want to, and must, explore that culture. (1986, p. 14)

6. These insights involve discerning what is good and bad about both traditional Aboriginal cultures and invading cultures.

An important task of any theology is to discern what is true and valuable for God's people to learn. As we search our culture in the light of the Gospel of the suffering Christ, we must ascertain those things which are alien, as well as those things which are true to the

Gospel. In the past, unfortunately, we allowed the European missionaries, who did not know our culture, to determine what was alien to the Christian faith within our culture. Because they saw Christianity only through Western eyes, they rejected most of our Aboriginal culture, regarding it as pagan and as having no relevance for a developing Australian indigenous Christianity.

The time has come for Aboriginal, not Western, Christians to identify both the good and bad in our traditional culture, and discover where our God is in our recent experiences of oppression. It is also important that we, given our experiences of European and Western culture and religion, identify those features of European and Western Christianity which have alienated us from the very Gospel the missionaries were preaching.

One example of European misinterpretation of Aboriginal culture comes from George Rosendale. George's comments demonstrate how European evaluations of the Aboriginal Creator Spirit, Yiirmbal, are alien to his own understanding of his own culture and its God — a God who was always with people, walking around with them, looking after them, watching over them, and providing them with all they needed to live.

> White men said that Yiirmbal was always out to destroy people, that he was an angry God, a God of destruction and not a God of love. As far as I'm concerned that's rubbish. The God that our ancestors believed in is very much the same God that we [Christians] worship today. (1993, p. 3)

One of the workshop participants compared the Aboriginal experience of the Creator Spirit providing food and sustenance with the experience of the Israelites being sustained with manna in the wilderness. God guided our people to take just enough food for our daily needs and promised if we were not greedy, but shared what we found, there would always be enough for tomorrow.

7. The stream from the North represents the ancient wisdom of Christians who came to our land.

The symbol of the North in this model is the sheep. Europeans who came to this land brought with them the sheep, which became a major source of their wealth and power. In order to graze their sheep, these invaders took large tracts of Aboriginal land, cleared them and sowed them with foreign grasses.

The sheep was also the symbol of the people we were expected to be as Christians. From our childhood, we learned to sing:

I am Jesus' little lamb
therefore glad at heart I am.

We were also introduced to Jesus as the Good Shepherd, an image that has little meaning for us since we had no feeling for sheep. Furthermore, the landowners who herded the sheep did not give us a comforting image of shepherds!

Nevertheless, the European Christians also brought with them wisdom and truths from their history from which we too can learn as we do theology.

8. Rainbow Spirit Theology comes from two main sources in the North: the Bible and church history.

The Bible is also a key source of theology for Christian Aboriginal people. We accept that God has spoken and continues to speak through the Christian Scriptures. This God of the Scriptures is known to Aboriginal people as the Creator Spirit, who speaks to us through the land. The land is like the Scriptures — sacred stories and signs are inscribed on the landscape, and readily available for those who can read them.

'Take away our Scriptures and we die!' In that cry from one of the workshop participants, the deep anguish felt by our Aboriginal people in losing our story places in the land became evident. The suffering of Aboriginal people continues because we cannot walk the land to read our Scriptures as we once did.

There is much from the 2000 years of Christian tradition which is also of value for our theology. There is much, however, that has negated Aboriginal people's experience of ourselves and our culture, and therefore must be judged as alien to the Gospel.

The North as a source of theology needs to be examined critically. European Christians belonging to a Western culture viewed our Aboriginal culture as heathen and confused the Gospel with their own Western culture. Christian Aboriginal people must now discern Christ in our culture and reclaim the Gospel in the light of our culture.

9. We get our bearings for doing this theology from the East. Christ, the revelation of God the Creator Spirit, guides us as we do our theology. The Gospel message of Jesus Christ, the crucified and risen Lord, gives us our bearings as we do our Rainbow Spirit Theology.

In Western culture, which has been traditionally located in the northern hemisphere, bearings are frequently determined by orienting towards the North; the North Pole and the North Star have been symbols of what determines people's bearings. In Aboriginal culture, the East rather than the North orients our people as we travel over the land. Direction is determined by the movement of the sun across the sky. We determine our bearings from the East, from the sunrise.

The Gospel is the sun in the East, the message of Christ as the full revelation of God the Creator Spirit in our time. Rainbow Spirit Theology is good news for our people. The Gospel gives us our Christian Aboriginal theological bearings. Our theology must be consistent with the message of the Gospel and reflect the Spirit of Christ at work within us. The risen Christ is the risen Son; Jesus Christ is our new life, our new dawn. Christ is our morning star.

The symbol of the East is the kookaburra who, as the first among the birds, announces the coming of the sun at dawn. The kookaburra symbolises the good news, and is our symbol of the Gospel which orients our theology.

Among Aboriginal people, there are many stories

about birds and animals. One kookaburra story, told by one of the workshop participants, emphasises the power of the kookaburra as the best singer of all the birds:

> In the beginning, the elders met to choose the bird who would sing their ceremonies. They needed a bird with a powerful and beautiful voice to sing the ceremony strong.
>
> They first invited Parrot to sing. But Parrot's voice was too sharp and piercing. Next they invited Mopoke, but his voice was too deep and unhappy. Then they invited Cockatoo, but her voice screeched too much.
>
> Finally they invited Kookaburra to sing. Kookaburra's voice was rich, strong and cheerful. So Kookaburra was chosen to announce and sing the ceremonies.

10. Rainbow Spirit Theology understands this Gospel not as a message limited to God saving souls for heaven, but as a message of God in Christ freeing all creation.

We do not understand the Gospel in a narrow sense which focuses exclusively on rescuing souls from personal sin and arranging their transfer to heaven. Christ came to redeem lives, communities and, ultimately, all creation from all the forces of evil at work in the world.

Life for us means life on the land. To point to heaven as our homeland and therefore to deny our spiritual life-connection with this land is to deny our very identity and our spiritual nature.

As one of the workshop participants said: 'I feel a deep spiritual connection with the land. When that connection is broken I suffer. Has Christ come to break that connection, or to restore it?'

Another participant added that if the younger generation of Aboriginal peoples is to be saved, the older generation must rediscover everything it can about past culture. 'Knowing our past culture restores and renews us. It is the land that connects us with each other. It is God who teaches us about the land.'

One outcome of the European missionaries' preaching of a narrow Gospel is reflected in the common quote: 'While European missionaries were pointing our eyes to heaven above, their European brothers were stealing the land from under our feet below.' Or, as another participant said: 'Before we said "Amen", our land was gone!'

11. The stream to the West represents hope for the future, and strength for the people who live this theology to affirm their Aboriginality as Christian. Rainbow Spirit Theology is a possible future, a new direction for Christian Aboriginal people.

The West is the direction in which the sun and our lives are moving. The West represents the answer for the future, a theology to strengthen our people for the future.

This discussion of Rainbow Spirit Theology is only the beginning. Hopefully it will inspire others to be proud of their Aboriginality and find new spiritual hope in developing a theology which affirms their own Aboriginal heritage. Rainbow Spirit Theology is intended to free Aboriginal Christians from European ways that hinder their discovery of what the Gospel of Christ means in their lives.

The symbol of the West is the kangaroo. The kangaroo never jumps backwards but moves relentlessly forward to reach the goal. This is a story, told by one of the workshop group, about how the kangaroo discovered the answer to his need.

> One time, long ago, Kangaroo was a man. He was very nice looking, a smart fellow. He thought he was better than other young men. For this, nobody liked him. He was lonely and had no mates.
>
> One day he decided to go away and get away from it all. So he left, and started walking along

the beach to the tribes living in the north. As he was walking along, he saw something floating on the water. First he thought it was a crocodile, but then when he looked again, he noticed it was coming closer with the tide, and it wasn't a crocodile. He waited for the tide to deposit it at his feet, so he could see what it was.

When it came ashore, he saw it was only a piece of driftwood. He picked it up, had a good look at it, and said, 'I'm going to make use of this stick!' He put it on his head, but he found he couldn't go forward through the bush. So he pulled it off and tried it on his tummy — but he couldn't bend down to eat. He pulled it off and tried it on his backside. He jumped, and tried again and again, and decided to keep it.

So, to this day, you see the kangaroo hopping across the plains, happy and complete, and with many friends.

12. The way to the West represents an open invitation for all Australians to do theology, to discern the voice of God in Australian Aboriginal culture and celebrate the Gospel in Aboriginal language and culture.

Doing theology also involves taking into account the context and audience for the theology. In the first instance, our theology is for Christian Aboriginal people.

Ultimately, however, it is also the voice of the Creator Spirit addressed to all Australians.

If the Gospel is to be expressed fully in the wider Australian context, it needs to take into account the voice of God now being discerned in our Aboriginal culture by Aboriginal people.

Aboriginal culture, Aboriginal spirituality and the Aboriginal experience of the Gospel are not to be viewed as curios of mission history, but as integral to the work of God in Australia. As such, they cannot be ignored by any who wish to preach the Gospel, or do theology, in Australia today. Our voice, the voice of indigenous Aboriginal theology, has a major contribution to make to all theology in Australia.

One workshop participant understood Pope John Paul as saying, on his recent visit to Alice Springs, that Aboriginal Christians are to be encouraged to explore their Aboriginal culture as a way of making a major contribution to the life and theology of the church in Australia.

The Rainbow Spirit within the Land with the Rainbow Above

chapter three

LAND AND CULTURE

1. In the very beginning, the earth was formless and empty of life. The Creator Spirit, in the form of the Rainbow Spirit, shaped the land, its mountains, seas, rivers and trees.

Among Aboriginal groups across Australia, there are power-filled stories about the earth in the very beginning. Some of these stories depict the earth as a vast featureless plain or desert until the Rainbow Spirit transforms it into the land we know today. In other stories, the earth is covered with water or mud prior to creation taking place.

These images in our stories are essentially the same as those depicted in Genesis 1:2 and 2:4. In the beginning the earth is specifically designated as formless and empty (*tohu wabohu*) but covered with water. Likewise, in

Genesis 2:4, the earth is depicted as a vast desert without life or form. (A discussion of land in Genesis 1 and 2 is given in the appendices.)

In these Genesis texts, and in the stories mentioned above, the focus is not on 'creation out of nothing' (*creatio ex nihilo*), though this belief appears elsewhere in the Christian Scriptures. The focus in these stories is rather on the transformation of a lifeless and empty earth into an ordered land and sea, filled with life.

2. From the beginning, the Rainbow Spirit has been and still is present deep within the land.

For most Aboriginal peoples in Australia, the Rainbow Spirit is linked closely to the land or the sea. Among some groups, the Rainbow Spirit emerges from the land and returns into the land where the Spirit's power is eternally present. This Spirit is always as close as the land. Aboriginal people believe the Rainbow Spirit left prints on the land, and each mark is a reminder of the Rainbow Spirit's promise to return from the land.

This image of God is unlike the one portrayed by many missionaries, who presented God as dwelling at a distance, living in heaven in splendid isolation. Prayers and songs were specifically directed to 'God in heaven', even though there was a belief that God was supposed to be everywhere. Most early missionaries did not discern either that God was present in the land of Australia, or the high level of spirituality that was present in our Aboriginal culture long before they appeared.

3. This Creator Spirit is known to Aboriginal Australians by many names, including Yiirmbal, Biame, Rainbow Spirit, Paayamu, Biiral, Wandjina and, in Christian times, Father God. In some traditions, the Creator Spirit and the Rainbow Spirit share the same name (for example, Yiirmbal).

The various images of the Creator Spirit among different Aboriginal peoples are quite diverse. Some of these beings assume particular forms when they function as creators: Wandjina is depicted on cave walls as a spirit without a mouth; in many of our traditions, the Rainbow Spirit is depicted as a massive snake whose creative powers transform the earth.

Behind all of these forms, however, we Christian Aboriginal people believe there is one Creator Spirit, who, in the Old Testament, is variously depicted as the Canaanite Creator, El Elyon, and as the Israelite Redeemer God, YHWH. (For details on El Elyon, see the discussion on land in the Abraham stories in the appendices.)

4. The Rainbow Spirit is the life-giving power of the Creator Spirit active in the world. The Creator Spirit filled the land with numerous life-forces and spiritual

forces. The Creator Spirit causes these life-forces to emerge from the land and its waters as plants, animals, fish and birds.

Aboriginal people believe the land is alive within, filled with the life-forces of all the species on earth. The land is itself alive, dynamic and creative. As Patrick Dodson said:

> The land is a living place made up of sky, clouds, rivers, trees, the wind, the sand; and the Spirit has planted my own spirit there, in my own country. It is something — and yet it is not a thing — it is a living entity. It belongs to me, I belong to it. I rest in it. I come from there. (1973)

The belief that life-forces are present within the land, and emerge at the impulse of the Creator Spirit, is consistent with the picture presented in Genesis 1. According to the imagery in this chapter of Genesis, all vegetation and animal life emerge from the land at the summons of God.

We Aboriginal Australians believed that by performing rites at sacred places, we were cooperating with the Creator Spirit in replenishing the earth. For many Aboriginal people, this human–divine cooperation is still a daily occurrence, concretely epitomised in each individual's birth. As one person at the workshop said: 'Three people cooperated to bring me into the world: my mother, my father and Yiirmbal, the Creator Spirit.'

*Life-forces from the Rainbow Spirit Emerging
from Sacred Sites in the Land*

5. Human beings are also created from the land by the Creator Spirit, and eventually return to that Spirit, who is present in the land.

The spirit of human beings comes from the Creator Spirit and returns to the Creator Spirit. As one workshop participant said:

> When a person dies, the land, as mother, opens her womb and takes the body. But the spirit is not

in the land. Only the shell, the body, stays in the land; the spirit goes to Yiirmbal, the Rainbow Spirit.

Aboriginal people believe that the spirit of each person is sacred and belongs to the Creator Spirit. As George Rosendale writes:

> This is why the spirit is so sacred to man because it belongs to Yiirmbal. Before Aboriginal people would not commit suicide. The hangings we hear about in jail are new to Aborigines because Aborigines would never destroy that life. That life is Yiirmbal's; it is sacred in the human person.
> (1993, p. 5)

Genesis 2 emphasises that the spirit of the human being is breath from the Creator and belongs to the Creator. The preceding quote from Patrick Dodson emphasises that, for Aboriginal people, the Creator Spirit not only gives life and spirit to the human being, but locates the spirit of each person in a place which becomes that individual's 'country'. We believe that the spirit of a person, as much as the body, is therefore linked to the land.

This linking of the spirit with one's own country is illustrated by the story one person at the workshop tells of his birth. When his mother gave birth to him under a particular tree far from their home country, she deliberately placed her afterbirth and his umbilical cord in the ground. This act not only marked the place as sacred for her son, but also enabled the spirit, through the blood in the ground, to travel back through the land to their 'home country', and to link her son with his spiritual origins.

6. Human beings are entrusted with the responsibility to cooperate with the Creator Spirit both to care for and to activate the life-forces within the land.

Traditional Aboriginal people have a deep sense of responsibility for the welfare of the land entrusted to our care. The Creator Spirit is the true landowner, and human beings are like trustees, responsible to the Creator Spirit for the care of this land. A similar sense of responsibility to serve and sustain the land is reflected in Genesis 2:15. (See the discussion of land in Genesis 1 and 2 in the appendices.)

For Aboriginal people, this responsibility also extends to sustaining the life-forces in the land. We see ourselves as co-creators with the Creator Spirit, performing rites and actions which activate and sustain all life on the land. It is a complete misunderstanding to call our religion some kind of pagan fertility religion. Rather, we believe that the Creator Spirit has given us the spiritual task of sustaining the life-forces of the earth for the blessing of all peoples. In the *burn-time* ceremony, a renewing ceremony, the caretakers and custodians of the land cooperate with the Creator Spirit who comes to the land to bless the land, to enable it to produce food. In this ceremony, sections of the land are burnt by the elders. Dew on the grass in the morning is a sign that the Creator Spirit has visited and blessed the land.

Many Aboriginal people are broken by their shame and guilt at not being able to fulfil this sacred responsibility. We believe the Creator Spirit still teaches Aboriginal people land-care through our living on and with the land.

7. In the beginning, the Creator Spirit entrusted different lands to different peoples. To Aboriginal Australians, this Spirit entrusted the land of Australia and its waters. The Creator Spirit is the true owner of the whole land and its waters.

Aboriginal people know from the Creator Spirit, and from the land itself, that we are responsible for sustaining the land of Australia. The land from which we came, where our afterbirth is buried, is given us in trust. To breach that trust is to violate the law of the Creator Spirit, written in and on the land.

Christian Aboriginal people point to key texts of the Scriptures as evidence that the God of the Bible confirms our belief that we are the ones given the various parts of Australia as the places for which we are responsible out of all the lands on the earth. Especially significant is Acts 17:26–27 (NRSV):

> From one ancestor he made all nations to inhabit
> the whole earth, and he allotted the times of their

existence and the boundaries of the places where
they would live, so that they would search for
God and perhaps grope for him and find him —
though indeed he is not far from each one of us.

We believe that the land of Australia is the land once allotted to Aboriginal Australians, not to the European invaders. We Aboriginal Australians therefore believe that the land of Australia is still in our trust and it is our responsibility to sustain the land. We are responsible to the Creator Spirit for the land and its bounty. The Creator Spirit is the true owner of the land and its waters.

Some Christian Aboriginal people point to the story of the Tower of Babel as further biblical support for our belief that the culture and land of Australia are God-given. This story in Genesis ends with people being given different languages and moving off to different locations as a result of God's intervention. Language is a bearer of all culture; the Aboriginal languages are no less bearers of culture than the languages of other lands.

8. Specific areas of the land are entrusted into the care of specific groups. These groups are the custodians of the land, its laws, its stories, its resources, its families, its ceremonies and its sacred sites.

The land as a whole belongs to the Creator Spirit, who gave it to Aboriginal people to look after as trustees. We do not own the land but we are responsible for its care.

The Creator Spirit gave to each group a particular area for which that group is responsible.

Each Aboriginal group has a sacred place in the land and a sacred song about its land. At this sacred place we perform our ceremonies, singing our songs and dancing our dances. These ceremonies are part of our responsibility as custodians of the land: they ensure that we preserve our connections with the Creator Spirit, that we maintain the resources and life-forces of the land, and that we keep alive the law and culture given us by our ancestors.

Aboriginal groups are linked with each other throughout the land. The land unites us as one. Our territories are marked by the trails of our common ancestors. Wherever we travel we find people with whom we are connected.

9. The identity of Aboriginal peoples is determined by their deep connection with the land; for many, these connections in the land are linked with their personal Dreaming sites, stories and totems. All these connections link people to the Creator Spirit.

In each Aboriginal person there is land and spirit. Both of these link each one of us with the land and the Creator Spirit in the land. For us Aboriginal people to know our true identity, it is vital for us to know the specific place in the land to which we belong.

For each of us, this place is our place of origin, our

personal story place — or, as some would say, our personal Dreaming site. Each place connects us with the land as our spiritual home. This site and this story also links us with a creature or a part of creation with which we have a common spiritual link. A common spiritual life-force links us with our story, our place, and this living symbol, which some refer to as our totem.

All of these spiritual parts of our world link us with the Creator Spirit, who gives life and strength to all things.

10. The ancestors walked the land, also filling it with spiritual forces. These forces are concentrated in sacred sites throughout the land. These sacred sites include fertility sites, conception sites, initiation sites, and cremation and burial sites.

To Aboriginal people, the land is not spiritual in some vague or general way. In specific sacred places, particular spiritual forces are present. These spiritual forces are linked with our spirit-filled ancestors who walked the land. Wherever they walked, they left a trail of life-forces. And at the places where they went into the ground, their spiritual presence is concentrated in a special way at a sacred site.

Each sacred site is a place where spiritual forces are concentrated. These forces link that site with the beginning, our ancestors and the Creator Spirit. Our elders are the custodians of these sites and must tend them according to sacred law.

Especially significant for our Aboriginal identity are those sites which link us with our personal story and those creatures with which we have a personal spiritual connection. These living symbols, or totems, establish kinship and connections with other members of the group. Aboriginal people who do not know their personal totem or story place feel they have lost their spiritual roots. When we meet, Aboriginal people ask each other, 'What is your dreaming? What is your story?' and, in some contexts, 'What is your totem?'

It is through the Creator Spirit that each of us has a connection. That personal connection with the beginning, or as some would say, with the Dreaming, tells us who we are spiritually. The Creator Spirit enters each of us so that we can tell our story. Our stories are not like the history-based stories of the Israelites. Our stories are the creation stories through which the Creator Spirit has given us our spiritual identity in our land.

11. The Creator Spirit renews the land, and through the land teaches land-care to its custodians. Family and social structures are also connected with the land by the Creator Spirit.

The Psalmist proclaims:

> When you send forth your spirit, they are created;
> and you renew the face of the ground.
>
> (Psalm 104:30, NRSV)

We proclaim the same truth when we recognise the Creator Spirit renewing the land. The Creator Spirit activates the life-forces in the land to bring nature to life. The same Spirit activates the spiritual forces in the land to give life to human beings. The Creator Spirit is a God of all life and fertility.

The Creator Spirit leaves signs in the land which teach its custodians how to tend the land. The sacred law from the Creator Spirit also specifies rituals in which custodians cooperate with the Creator Spirit to activate the life-forces in the land. Every day, many Aboriginal people are still cooperating with the Creator Spirit by the way we walk through, live with, talk about and care for the land.

Chapter four

LAND AND CRYING

1. The Creator Spirit is crying because the deep spiritual bonds with the land and its people have been broken. The land is crying because it is slowly dying without this bond of spiritual life. The people are crying because they long for a restoration of that deep spiritual bond with the Creator Spirit and the land.

The suffering associated with the violation of our land is not a passing human pain. The Creator Spirit is suffering because of what has happened to the land.

The pain is like that of a parent losing a child. Many Aboriginal people do not realise that our suffering and pain are not caused by drink, drugs or city life, but is a result of our losing our spiritual connection with the land. When Aboriginal people are taken from our spiritual homes we also lose our spiritual contact with the Creator Spirit.

One workshop participant said: 'It tears me apart. I grieve with the Creator when I hear the land crying.' And we would add, the Creator Spirit grieves with us as the Creator grieved before the great flood (Genesis 6:6).

The suffering is spiritual, caused by the loss of our stories and songs which link us with our story places, ancestors and the Creator Spirit. The suffering is silent and deep, caused by the removal of Aboriginal people from our home country, where we are bound to the sacred place of our origin. The suffering is destructive, caused by the desecration of our sacred places and the removal of our ancient sacred stories once written in the landscape.

Our Spiritual Bonds with the Land Have Been Broken

Stealing our land is not like stealing a cow. Stealing our land means stealing our souls, stealing what is most precious and dear to us, stealing our freedom and the spiritual strength within us. Stealing our land means taking our lives. Stealing our land is murder.

And the land cries out because the blood of our murdered people has not been appeased.

2. The Creator Spirit is crying because the sacred places of the land have been desecrated. The land is crying because the stories and rites associated with these sacred places are being forgotten. The people are crying because they have lost the power to maintain their sacred places.

Highways have crossed the land and erased the trails of our ancestors. Mines have been dug deep into the land and desecrated our home countries. Cities have been constructed on sacred places where our stories once gave us strength and meaning. Farms have torn up the land where the Creator Spirit once provided plants and animals for our livelihood.

All of these activities of the European invaders have desecrated this land and made us, the original custodians of the land, dispirited refugees and outcasts in our own country. The land, we believe, is still crying out for its rightful custodians. And our people long once again to care for the land as the Creator Spirit intended. We are unable to fulfil our sacred responsibility towards the land and the Creator Spirit.

The pollution of Maralinga with atomic fallout illustrates the extent to which so-called civilised Europeans will go to exploit the land for their own benefit, with no respect or concern for the sacred land which they made barren. For thousands of years, we tended those Maralinga lands with great respect and care. In one evil act, Europeans made it totally barren.

3. The Creator Spirit is crying because the land is dispossessed. The land is crying because the people assigned by the Creator Spirit to be its custodians have been torn from the land by force. The people of the land are crying because they are unable to fulfil their responsibilities as custodians of the land.

The story of Naboth's vineyard in 1 Kings 21 is often cited by Christian Aboriginal people as a precedent and parallel to what has happened to Aboriginal people in Australia. Ahab, a rich and powerful king, wanted to acquire the vineyard of Naboth, an Israelite peasant. Naboth refused to sell, on the grounds that the vineyard was his ancestral land. He said: 'God forbid that I should sell my ancestral heritage' (verse 3, NRSV). Jezebel, Ahab's wife, devised a plan: Naboth was executed and Ahab acquired the land.

In a similar way, the powerful Europeans took lands from us. These lands, too, are our ancestral heritage. They were given to us in trust by God, through our ancestors. Our lands, for which we are responsible, are the lands of the Creator Spirit. They are our lands; it is our responsibility to care for them. The Europeans who took our land are as guilty as Ahab.

The prophet Elijah confronted Ahab with his crimes: murder and dispossession of ancestral lands. We, like Elijah, are called to confront European Australians with their crimes, the crimes of dispossessing indigenous peoples by force and murdering those who resisted.

Now that the land is dispossessed, our people who once cared for our ancestral lands have been deprived of their very reason for being. Our identity as custodians of the lands once given to us by our ancestors has been violated. As one workshop participant said: 'We now feel like strangers in our own land.' Aboriginal men, especially, feel shame before the Creator Spirit because they have failed in their attempts to protect their land.

4. The Creator Spirit is crying because the life-forces formed in the land are being destroyed. The land is crying because these life-forces are not bringing forth rich vegetation and abundant animal life. The people are crying because they are prevented from maintaining the law that once maintained this life.

The Creator Spirit is crying because the creative life-forces deep within the land are being destroyed. These life-forces reach back to our ancestors who walked the land and left their life-giving energy in the land. These life-forces also reach back to the Creator Spirit who filled the land with creative powers.

These life-forces are damaged and destroyed when the land is cleared of all its trees, when its water is polluted by industry, when its soil is defiled by over-farming, and when its face is scarred by sand-mining. Ecologists now recognise that the balance of life-forces in the land has been badly damaged, and in some cases destroyed forever. The abundance of animal and plant life we once knew is no longer found in our land. Many species of life we carefully tended are now extinct.

Our ancestors gave us the law, the Aboriginal law of the land. That law was about how to tend the land, to sustain the life-forces, to preserve the balance of life-forces, and to respect those life-forces as eternal gifts from our Creator Spirit.

It hurts us now to find the land devoid of the rich life we once knew. One workshop participant said:

> My spiritual link goes back to my ancestors in my country. When I drive through my country it hurts. It hurts to see bulldozers removing the life my ancestors gave us. I feel the pain of my ancestors when they see their country being raped and ripped apart. My heart cries when I see the land barren and empty.

Our elders who knew the law and were responsible for sustaining the life-forces of the land have been removed. We can no longer keep the law of the land and maintain our trust as custodians of the land. But we long to do so again.

5. The Creator Spirit is crying because the blood of Aboriginal people has desecrated the land. The land is crying out because the blood shed on the land has not been heard, and the sacrifice of those who died has not been remembered. The people are crying because the crimes committed against their ancestors have not been revealed and appropriately recognised.

The following catalogue of crimes committed against the Aboriginal peoples in this land is long and painful, and incomplete:

- the massacre of innocent Aboriginal groups by official government parties;
- the hunting down of Aboriginal people like wild animals;
- the poisoning of waterholes and streams to exterminate Aboriginal families;
- the desecration of sacred sites and Dreaming places;
- the forceful removal of women and children from their families;
- the humiliation of Aboriginal people with shameful public punishment;
- the sexual abuse of Aboriginal women by settlers and people associated with missions;
- the designation of Aboriginal human beings as sub-human or racially inferior;
- the imposition of Western customs that were tantamount to enslavement;
- the death of humiliated Aboriginal youths in custody;
- the vilification of Aboriginal spiritual life and worship as evil and barbaric.

The blood of our ancestors cries out in anguish, like the blood of Abel in Genesis 4. The land, too, cries because of the blood spilled on the earth. The cry is first of all for public recognition and confession. Yet these atrocities and deaths have not been recognised for what they are — atrocities.

Desecrated Monument remembering Aboriginal Massacres in the Region of Cloncurry

Australia has Anzac Day to remember the death of those who died fighting for this land on foreign shores. A day is set aside to remember the holocaust. Another day is set aside to remember Hiroshima. The public remember these events so that the evils perpetrated may never happen again. But the atrocities committed in our own land are ignored. The Aboriginal people who died fighting for their land are not remembered, their names are not even recorded, and their sacrifices are not recognised by most Aboriginal people or other Australian citizens.

As the historian Henry Reynolds writes:

> Twenty thousand blacks were killed before federation. Their burial mound stands out as a landmark of awesome size on the peaceful plains of colonial history. If the bodies had been white, our histories would be heavy with their story, a forest of monuments would celebrate their sacrifice . . . In parts of our continent the Aboriginal death toll overshadows even that of the overseas wars of the twentieth century. About 5000 Europeans from Australia north of the Tropic of Capricorn died in the five wars between the outbreak of the Boer War and the end of the Vietnam engagement. But in a similar period — say the 70 years between the first settlement in North Queensland in 1861 and the early 1930s — as many as 10 000 blacks were killed in skirmishes with the Europeans in north Australia. (1989, p. 22)

6. The Creator Spirit is crying because those bonds which linked people to the land and sustained family structures have also been broken. The land is crying because families no longer know where or how they are linked to the land. People are crying because families are broken and torn by the evils of an alien social order.

The painful crying of the Creator Spirit and our ancestors is not only provoked by the unwarranted desecration of sacred land or by the atrocities which have stained the landscape, but also by the cruel destruction of our Aboriginal way of life. The bonds which linked our people to the land, linked our people spiritually, linked our people in families, linked our people in local societies — these bonds have all been broken and our people are set adrift, torn from our world of meaning.

The breaking of these ties by the forceful imposition of Western religion and customs, laws and social structure is cultural genocide.

Our personal stories and story places gave us a personal and spiritual identity which fixed our place in our family, in our group and in Aboriginal society. By removing our people from our home country, this bond is severed. By destroying our story places and sacred sites, this bond is defiled. By forcing our people to change our names and adopt another culture, this bond is damaged, sometimes forever. Yet, in spite of this, we Aboriginal people keep searching for our home country, for our personal story places and for our bonds with our ancestors. For in these realities of our culture lie the roots of the spiritual identity which we once inherited as children.

7. The Creator Spirit is crying because the land and its people are in bondage to the Pharaoh of Western culture. The land is crying because it is not given the rest and respect which would enable it to be restored. The people are crying out to be free once again to be responsible for the land and make it free.

What has happened to Aboriginal people is a form of bondage to Western religion and culture, a bondage from which it is very difficult to be liberated. This bondage is represented by the Western ways, laws and power structures which prevent us from being ourselves and stop us living as free people on our lands. As one workshop participant said: 'I feel free when I go to my own country. I want all of my life to be free.'

As Christian Aboriginal people, we ask whether the Gospel, brought to us by the missionaries, is part of the culture which enslaved us, or whether the power of the Gospel frees us to be true to ourselves and our land.

The stories of how Western culture was forced upon people are heart-rending. One of the workshop group tells the story of how his mother was forced to leave her home country and her story place, forced to walk over 200 miles to Laura in far north Queensland, and then taken by rail to Cooktown, where she was expected to live in an offshore penal settlement, Palm Island. She was forced to speak only English even to her young child, a difficult task for someone straight from the bush. But she, like many mothers, resisted Western oppression and sought to preserve her culture. But when the officials heard her speaking her own language, they threw her into prison with her son, 'Bill', who was only five years old. (In line with this policy of assimilation, her child was given a European name, Bill.) Bill, who is now in his fifties, only discovered his Aboriginal name a few years ago.

As slaves to the European Australians, Aboriginal Australians contributed much to the wealth of the country. Our labours in the cane fields, on the railways, in the pearl industry, on cattle stations and in many other industries have never really been publicly acknowledged. Aboriginal labourers were virtual slaves, being paid in tobacco, flour, sugar or keep. Even today, many of our people are still slaves because we have neither the skills to compete in a mechanised society, nor the capacity to return to our home country and be free.

The land, too, is in slavery to Western forms of exploitation and control — which prevents the land from thriving with life as it once did under Aboriginal custodians. The land needs rest and care to be restored. The same principle of rest for the land is found in Leviticus 25, where the Sabbath law for the land is outlined for Israel (cf. 2 Chronicles 36:21).

Both the land and its people cry out for freedom. Will anyone hear our cry and treat our ongoing slavery as a serious injustice?

chapter five

LAND AND CHRIST

1. In the Christian Scriptures, God the Creator is depicted as creating all things in several ways. These include using Wisdom, the Word and the Spirit.

In the Book of Proverbs, Wisdom is said to be present with God before creation (Proverbs 8:22–31). God uses Wisdom to create the sky, the land and the waters that fertilise the land (Proverbs 3:19–20).

In Genesis 1, the Spirit of God is also present from before creation (Genesis 1:2). This Spirit is used by God to create life on earth and to renew the land (Psalm 104:27–30).

Especially important is the Word as the power God uses to create in Genesis 1 and in John 1. In John 1, the Word is described as follows:

> In the beginning was the Word, and the Word was
> with God, and the Word was God. He [the Word]
> was in the beginning with God. All things came
> into being through him, and without him not one
> thing came into being. (John 1:1–3, NRSV)

The Wisdom, the Spirit and the Word are three ways of depicting the creative power of God. In John 1:3–4, this life-giving power is simply called 'life'.

2. In our Aboriginal culture, the Creator Spirit is also depicted as creating things in various ways. These include the actions of the ancestor beings and especially the Rainbow Spirit.

Many Aboriginal people are conscious of the presence of the Creator Spirit in the land today. We believe that the creative power of the Creator Spirit has been creating and giving life since the beginning. That power continues to give life today. We also experience this spiritual power in sacred places as something awesome, a power which is to be respected by all.

We have many stories about how our ancestor spirits travelled the land and created the present landscape. One of the most powerful and common of these stories depicts the Rainbow Spirit as a powerful snake who forms parts of the land, and gives life to the land and all living creatures. We believe that all of these creative powers and stories come from the Creator Spirit and direct us back to the Creator Spirit.

For some of us, the Rainbow Spirit is an extension of the Creator Spirit. The two are one being and often have the same name. This is the mystery at the heart of our religion. Others feel that the Rainbow Spirit is one of the ancestor spirits and is not to be identified with God as the Creator Spirit. We all agree that we need to explore the stories of the Rainbow Spirit, each in our own country, to discover their meaning and mystery for our theology.

3. The mystery of the Creator Spirit was only partially revealed in the Old Testament and in our Aboriginal culture. Signs and symbols of this mystery, however, are found both in the Old Testament and in Aboriginal culture. The full revelation of this mystery is found in the person of Jesus Christ.

Missionaries frequently referred to actions and promises of God in the Old Testament which pointed forward to the coming of Christ. The God of the Old Testament is portrayed as the Creator. God's mighty word was the power God used to create the world and to give life to all things.

The action of God in redeeming the Israelites from slavery in Egypt, and giving them a land of their own, was presented as a Gospel message, typical of God's way of redeeming God's people. The promised land was presented as a place where God was revealed at sacred sites.

The land of Australia and the stories of its Aboriginal

peoples also offer clues about how the Creator Spirit brings life and hope. That same Creator Spirit gave this land to the Aboriginal peoples as a 'promised land' (Acts 17:26–27). This promised land was also filled with sacred sites where God has been revealed. Most missionaries, however, did not find these signs of the Creator Spirit in our culture. They did not ask us about our stories of the beginning, or about the power of the Creator Spirit which we knew about, and experienced in our lives.

4. The life-giving power of the Creator Spirit was always close to our people. We believe that this power took on human flesh in Jesus Christ, and fulfilled the searchings of the people of the Old Testament and of Aboriginal people.

The Creator Spirit was not only present giving life to the land, but was also close at hand, giving spiritual life to all Aboriginal people. The close presence of this spiritual power was experienced in our Aboriginal way of life and our ceremonies. The presence of this power among Aboriginal people pointed to the special presence of that power in the person of Jesus Christ.

We Aboriginal people, like the Israelites, sought to understand the mystery of the Creator Spirit among us. These searchings were fulfilled when we discovered that the life-giving power of the Creator Spirit had become a human being in Jesus Christ. In Jesus Christ, the life-giving power of the Creator Spirit was revealed in a way never before experienced by the peoples of any culture.

5. When the life-giving Creator Spirit took human form, God camped among us as a human being; God became one of us in our land, and became part of our culture.

The way John's Gospel describes the life-giving power of the Creator Spirit taking on human form is especially meaningful for Aboriginal people. John 1:14 reads: 'The Word (*logos*) became flesh and tabernacled among us and we beheld his glory.'

Three elements in this passage demand special attention. When the *logos*, the mysterious creative Word and power of God, became a human being, this is described as God pitching a tent or tabernacle. In Aboriginal terms, God 'camped' among us. God built a humpy among us. And God's camp among us is human flesh.

Some of us would identify this life-giving power of God, who became a human being among us, as the life-giving power of the Rainbow Spirit and of our ancestor spirits. In Jesus Christ, we see the true nature of the Rainbow Spirit as a life-giving God of love, and not as an awesome power that frightens us. For others, the Rainbow Spirit is not the same as God or the Word made flesh in Jesus Christ, but is one of our creative ancestors.

The second point about this passage is that the form which the Creator Spirit assumes is described as 'flesh'. It is not Jewish flesh, or even European flesh. The emphasis is on God assuming a human form, common to all of us. We are all flesh and blood, like Jesus Christ.

A third point to be noted about this text is the reference to God's glory: the mysterious, powerful and awesome presence of God, which was experienced by God's people in Old Testament times. A similar mysterious and awesome presence of God, the Creator Spirit, has long been experienced by Aboriginal people in our sacred places and ceremonies.

Now that awesome presence of God is seen in the person of Jesus Christ. The Creator Spirit, the God of creation, is revealed in Christ to be the Reconciling Spirit, the God of redemption and liberation.

By camping among us as a human being in a form common to all of us, God has become one of us. As one of us, Christ is in our camp, in our land, and is part of our culture.

Our Aboriginal Christ

6. This means that for Aboriginal Australians, Christ is revealed not as a German Jesus, an English Jesus, or even a Jewish Jesus, but as an Aboriginal Jesus.

If God in Christ is indeed one of us, then for Aboriginal peoples, Christ is an Aboriginal Australian, not an alien or foreign human being whom we cannot know. The Gospel message is that God has become a human being like us.

The full import of this Gospel message for us as Aborigines can only be understood when we remember that the life-giving power from the Creator Spirit has been and remains present in the land (see Hebrews 1:1–2; 2:1–3). We believe the land is alive with the spiritual presence of the Creator Spirit; the land is an extension of the Creator Spirit and filled with life-giving power. We belong to the land as we belong to the Creator Spirit.

By assuming human form, the life-giving spirit of the land enters human flesh. We express something of the depth of this mystery if we say that in Christ 'the spiritual presence in the land becomes flesh and camps among us'. This Christ is truly Aboriginal. When Aboriginal people become Christians, we believe the power of the Holy Spirit takes us back to our Aboriginal culture and beliefs, and back to the life-giving power of the Creator Spirit.

7. In Jesus Christ we see the mystery, the victory and the love of God fully revealed. Most missionaries kept that revelation partially hidden because they presented

Christ as a European Jesus who had little or no kinship with Aboriginal culture.

During the workshops, we frequently expressed our sorrow over the way many missionaries derided our Aboriginal beliefs and customs, describing them as 'heathen' and 'rubbish'. These same missionaries demanded that we Aboriginal people accept a Jesus who was portrayed as a European. The simple pictures of Jesus they showed to us, the songs they sang to us, and the customs they brought to us were alien to Aboriginal culture.

> As George Rosendale wrote in an unpublished paper:
> St Paul's approach to the 'heathens' was different to how the missionaries approached the Aboriginals. The words 'heathen' and 'rubbish' were two strong words the missionaries used against our religion and beliefs. Paul pointed the people to the True God and Jesus Christ as the crucified Lord and risen Saviour. What he taught and said was left to the Holy Spirit; then Paul moved on to other people and places.

We, as Aboriginal Christians, are now asserting that, in spite of the missionaries, the Holy Spirit has been among us and was leading us to know that Christ is indeed one of us, an Aboriginal person 'camping' among us, giving life to our people and our stories.

It is not our intention in this outline of Rainbow Spirit Theology to discuss the redeeming work of Christ in detail. We affirm the Gospel message which proclaims the good news of redemption for all. Christ's victory over sin, death and evil is for all. At the same time, Djiniyini Gondarra declares:

> We Aboriginal leaders are called to plant Christ in this Aboriginal Australian 'fertile soil', rather than transplant our Western forms of Christianity . . . We must promote Christ as a living and acceptable part of our own ceremony and culture. Our confidence is that Christ has won the victory over all principalities and powers and that this victory will certainly become manifest if He is given the chance to do battle. (1986, p. 21)

8. By becoming one of us, the Creator Spirit through Jesus Christ frees us to affirm our past culture, including our deep connections with our land and our ancestors.

Christ, through his suffering, death and victory over evil, has made us free and continues to make us free. Christ liberates us from all forces that would enslave us. These forces are not only our personal sins but include the sins of others which have enslaved us, including the sins of Europeans who bound us to their culture and imprisoned us in locations far from our home country.

The Creator Spirit, through our Aboriginal Christ, frees us to begin the journey back to discover the good in our culture, and to discern the presence of the Creator Spirit in our ancestors' stories and in our land. We are now free to worship Christ in our own way. Christ was first revealed to us as the life-giving power of the Creator Spirit, and is now revealed to us more fully in the life, death and resurrection of Jesus Christ.

9. When Jesus Christ died, he was buried in the land and returned to the Creator Spirit. When he arose, he sent his Spirit to fill the land and make all things new, including our people.

*The Spirit of Christ Rises from the Land
to Renew our People and our Land*

Burial ceremonies are very important for Aboriginal people. We make sure our people are properly returned to our ancestors and to the Creator Spirit. When Jesus died, he too returned to the Creator Spirit, and, as some of us would say, to our ancestors.

But the Spirit of Christ did not remain in the land. Jesus rose again and sent his life-giving Spirit into the world. That Spirit of Christ now fills the world and makes things new (Colossians 3:9–10; Romans 6:3–4; 8). For us that means that the Spirit of Christ is making the land new.

In a special way, Christ's Spirit enters each one of us who believes. One participant was ready to make the following statement, though not all of us agreed:

> When Christ's Spirit lives in us as human beings, it is like the way the ancestor spirits lived in our totems. That means that the totem of Christ is not an animal or a bird but human beings. We Christians are Jesus' totems. We bear Jesus' image, the true image of God. Jesus is our true spiritual ancestor. 'By this shall all people know that you are my totem' (John 13:35).

chapter six

LAND AND RECONCILIATION

1. The Creator Spirit camped among us in Jesus Christ, who suffered, died and returned to life in our land.

The camping of Christ among us is a reality we Aboriginal people must face boldly. We have been strongly influenced by many Christian missionaries who emphasised that Christ is located first and foremost in cathedrals, churches or in European communities of faith. Missionaries and European pastors gave the impression they were 'bringing Christ' with them to our camps as a special favour. Their attitude was usually paternalistic.

But, as we said in the previous chapter, Christ as the life-giving power of the Creator Spirit has been camping among us since the beginning. Now that we understand the Creator Spirit has camped with us in a special way, assuming human flesh in the person of Jesus Christ, we need to claim Christ as one of us, as Aboriginal. And we need to declare that the suffering, death and resurrection of Christ are not only acts of history in a distant land, but living realities in our land. Christ suffers, dies and rises among us.

2. The Christ who suffered on the cross continues to suffer with the land and the people of the land. In the suffering of the land and the people of the land, we see Christ suffering and we hear Christ crying out.

In chapter 4 we described how the land has suffered. The land is crying because of the evils brought by those Europeans who invaded this land. We Aboriginal people of the land are also crying because of the evils and injustices committed against us. And our cries call out to God, the Creator Spirit in the land.

The suffering of Christ continues in the camps and homes of our rural and urban Aboriginal people across the land. When our Aboriginal people suffer and die with our land, Christ suffers and dies. The land cries: 'My God! My God! Why have you forsaken me?' The cry of the land is the cry of Christ, echoing through the ages, as Christ continues to suffer with us and for us.

The voice of God is heard from the midst of this suffering. It is the voice of the Creator Spirit in the land and in the camp. It is the voice of Christ announcing afresh: 'I am with you. I am suffering. I am here to give you new life.'

For our Australian theology to be true, we need to recognise not only that the land has suffered, but that God has suffered, and continues to suffer with the land and the people of this land.

3. The suffering land is the groaning creation referred to in the New Testament. Christ came among us to overcome the powers under which the suffering land is groaning. The evil which Christ overcomes is not only personal sin, but the forces which enslave people in society and in the environment in which we live.

'We know that the whole creation has been groaning in labor pains until now' (Romans 8:22, NRSV). (This text from Romans 8 is discussed in the appendices.)

We Aboriginal people of Australia have experienced this suffering of the land personally. We understand the land's bondage to the sins and evil forces imposed by many European invaders. We know the land has been sinned against. And we groan with the land as it, too, longs to be free of its bondage.

We believe, however, not only that Christ suffers with the land and our people, but that Christ can overcome the evils which enslave this land. The Christ who suffers is also the Christ who redeems and frees the land. Christ, who is the power of the Creator Spirit in human form, comes to free both our people and the land so that both can begin to live as the Creator Spirit intended.

Many missionaries oriented us Aboriginal people to heaven to save us from our sins, and ignored or were powerless to prevent the sins committed against our people and our land. Unfortunately, we still hear some Christians saying: 'Do not worry about your land; our promised land is in heaven.'

For salvation to be meaningful to Aboriginal people, we need to know that Christ died and rose to redeem the whole creation. From our understanding of the message of Paul to the Romans, we believe that Christ is the one who comes to us to redeem both us and our land.

4. Through Christ, the land and the people are reconciled with the Creator Spirit.

The crying of the land reflects barriers and broken relationships between the land and the peoples of the land. We Aboriginal people have been torn from our home country and many of us have lost our story places. We have become estranged from our own land and many of us have lost our spiritual connections with the land. We have become alienated from the Creator Spirit.

Christ, who suffers with the land, is present to bring us back to the land, and to the Creator Spirit within the land. Christ announces that he can overcome the evils which separate us from God, our Creator Spirit. That means that we can be at peace with the Creator Spirit and are free to discover the Spirit's power and presence in the land.

5. Through Christ we have the strength to be reconciled to each other and to the land. This means we are involved with Christ in the process of breaking down the barriers that divide Australian Aboriginal peoples from each other and from other Australians in this land.

Paul declares that Christ is the power of God which broke down the dividing wall of hostility which existed between the Jews and the Gentiles of his day. According to Paul:

> [Christ] is our peace; in his flesh he has made both groups into one and has broken down the dividing wall, that is, the hostility between us.
> (Ephesians 2:14, NRSV)

Christ, who has broken down this wall, is among us now to break down the dividing wall which separates Aboriginal Australians from other Australians in this country. Through Christ we can be one. Through the suffering of Christ we can be reconciled. And that process of healing has begun. Christ is calling us, inviting us to be a part of that healing, that reconciliation.

The Old Testament also points to the coming of a Christ who would bring spiritual life and reconciliation with God. Only with the coming of Jesus as the Christ was the full import of Christ's reconciling power revealed to European and Aboriginal peoples. Stories of reconciliation in our Aboriginal culture also prepare for this message.

George Rosendale tells one story about the black and white cockatoos, and how reconciliation was effected among them.

The cockatoos were brothers who lived long ago. When they became men, the black cockatoo realised he was different. He did not like it. He became very angry with his father because he made him black. He decided to change the way things were. One day he was found by his brother the white cockatoo, sitting under a tree, very upset and angry. 'What is the matter with you, my brother?' he asked.

'I'm very angry with my father,' he answered. 'He made you white and he made me black. I don't like it. I'm going to change my colour.'

He went to his uncle who lived over the range. He asked him for honey and clay. His uncle gave him what he wanted. He took the clay and made it into powder; then he put the honey all over himself and sprinkled the powdered clay over the honey. He looked at himself and said: 'Now I am like my brother.'

His grandfather, the storm bird, was very angry with the foolish brother. He called the North wind to bring rain. The monsoons came, and it rained and rained and rained, and washed all the clay and honey away.

Later, his brother found him again sitting under the tree, angry, sad and sorry for himself. He said, 'My brother, you did a foolish thing to hurt our father. We are his sons. He made both of us and he loves us. Come on, be happy! Our father loves you just as much as he loves me. We both belong to him. Be happy and rejoice.'

To this day the black cockatoos are happy. They even sing while flying and eating. (1988, p. 118)

George suggests that a story like this can illustrate the Gospel message of what Christ has done to make peace with God and with our fellow human beings. This story, he writes, provides a guide for interpreting passages like 1 Timothy 2:5 and John 14:16.

6. For the work of reconciliation in Christ to be effective, the Christian churches in Australia need to acknowledge the crimes committed against Aboriginal people, their culture and their land; seek reconciliation; and work with Aboriginal people in their struggles for justice.

The inhuman crimes committed against Aboriginal people, our culture and our land are now on public record. They can no longer be hidden. They can no longer be ignored as the irrelevant acts of European pioneers. The non-indigenous people in this country, including Christians, are the heirs of these evils.

If there is to be genuine reconciliation in this land, non-indigenous Christians need to have the courage, in Christ, to make public confession of past and present crimes against us, their Aboriginal brothers and sisters.

This confession needs to be more than a quiet liturgy hidden in the churches. It needs to be a bold public ritual, at appropriate times and places, to confront the rest of Australia with the ugly reality of its past sins against us, the Aboriginal people of this land.

This confession, to be recognised as genuine, needs to be followed by specific acts of involvement by Christian churches which seek to redress the wrongs and make restoration. The response of Zacchaeus was seen as genuine when he announced that he would restore fourfold anything he had stolen (Luke 19:1–8).

7. Christ strengthens us Aboriginal people to confront the Western-oriented church with the cry of God's people throughout history: 'Let my people go!' Reconciliation between peoples is only possible when people are free and equal.

We believe, in the light of our understanding of the Gospel presented above, that Christ frees us to return to our culture, our stories and our Creator Spirit. We contend that the European majority of the Christian Church has enslaved us in a Western version of Christianity which is not our own. We believe that we are now empowered by the suffering and resurrection of Christ to discern Christ's presence in our culture and the presence of the Creator Spirit in our land.

We believe we are free in Christ to proclaim Christ in terms of our own culture. Rainbow Spirit Theology is an expression of that freedom.

Appendix 1

The Land and the Beginning: Comments on Genesis 1 and 2

Most interpretations of Genesis 1 and 2 in print reflect the orientation of Western scholars and their history. If we read Genesis 1 and 2 from the perspective of indigenous Aboriginal theology, what fresh insights do we gain into the meaning of the text? More particularly, if we focus on the image of the land in these texts, what do we discover?

At the outset, we need to recognise that the Hebrew term *'ereṣ* can be translated 'earth' or 'land'. Similarly the term *shamayim* can be rendered 'heaven' or 'sky'. It is clear from Genesis 1:10 that *'ereṣ* in this chapter refers to land, and from verse 8 that *shamayim* refers to sky.

'Land' and 'sky' are terms which make immediate sense to the Aboriginal community. By using a term such as 'heaven', we introduce connotations of the abode of God as being above, ideas which are not necessarily implied in the text and are alien to Aboriginal culture.

So, in the light of these insights, we can begin the chapter with the translation,

> In the beginning, when God made the sky and the land, the land was formless and empty.

The image of the land as formless and empty is found in numerous Aboriginal creation stories about the land at the very beginning. In these stories, the land is transformed from its formless and empty state into the present landscape by the Creator Spirit or the ancestors.

In Genesis 1:2, the land is already there — but unformed and devoid of life. Also present, above and below, are waters, here called 'the deep'. It is clear from verses 9 and 10 that the land is located under these waters, and is not as yet exposed to sight, or in a form we would recognise. When God separates the land from the waters, the land comes up and is visible.

This image of the land as a given, waiting to be transformed into land and sea as we now know them, is also typical of the picture of 'land at the beginning' in Aboriginal dreaming stories. This image challenges the view commonly held by scholars, who have been greatly influenced by the Babylonian myth in which creation of land is one of the results of a battle against the forces of chaos. For these scholars, the chaos image is behind this passage in Genesis.

In the context of Rainbow Spirit Theology, there is no reason to import the concept of chaos at the beginning as integral to the text. The imagery of verse 2 makes excellent sense as land covered with water, waiting for the Creator Spirit, in whatever form, to commence transforming the scene.

The presence of the Creator Spirit at the beginning, which Aboriginal peoples have spoken about, and been aware of, for a long time, is also explicit in the text of Genesis. In the text, this power is spoken of as the breath, wind or Spirit of God. This Spirit moves over the waters which cover the land. Thus the Creator Spirit is present from the beginning, and is associated with transforming the unformed land.

The picture here is not one of a deity descending, in spectacular fashion, from some heavenly abode to create a world out of nothing. Rather, the Creator Spirit is portrayed as moving across, and closely linked with, the land from the beginning.

The portrait of God creating light and sky on the first two days of creation is not our concern at this time. The third day, when the land is transformed, however, requires special attention in our Rainbow Spirit Theology.

Land is not created out of nothing. Rather, at the summons of the Creator Spirit, the land lying beneath the waters 'appears'. The waters covering the land are gathered into seas, and the land appears from below as 'dry land'. Or, in the words of verse 9,

> Let the waters under the sky be gathered into one place, and let the dry land appear.

The verb 'appear' is especially important here. The form of the verb is used elsewhere, when God or an angel is revealed or 'appears'. The image is of the hidden land below 'appearing'. The land is thus a revelation, a manifestation that appears at the summons of God.

The image of the land as revelation is similar to the Aboriginal concept of the land as sacred and linked with the Creator Spirit from the beginning.

Not only is the hidden presence of the land revealed, however; hidden powers lying deep within the land are also revealed. God does not say, 'Let there be vegetation' but rather, 'Let the land bring forth vegetation' (verse 11). The life-forces of vegetation within the land emerge as plant life at the impulse of the Creator Spirit. The land is the reservoir of all plant life.

Similarly, in verse 20, the Creator Spirit summons the waters to 'bring forth' life, everything from the smallest creature to the great sea monsters.

Thus both the land and the sea are portrayed as bodies where life-forces are latent and from which they emerge as creatures, all the work of the Creator Spirit.

Even more striking, perhaps, is the fact that animal life, too, emerges from the land. This image is common in Aboriginal dreaming stories. Kangaroos, dingos, lizards and all animal life emerge from the land. Once again, in Genesis 1:24, God issues a summons to the land:

> Let the land bring forth living creatures of every
> kind, cattle and creeping things and wild animals
> of the land of every kind.

Thus every species of animal and insect life also emerges from the land. The land, it seems, held within it, from the beginning, the life-forces of these creatures; the Creator Spirit brings each into tangible form from the land.

Unlike animals and plants, human beings do not seem to emerge from the land in the same way. The Creator Spirit creates mortals in 'the image of God' as a distinct species accountable to God, and with the responsibility to 'rule over' all forms of life in the land, sea and air.

This is not the place to enter the ancient debate about the meaning of 'the image of God'. What is explicit here in this text is that human beings, as a consequence of being 'in God's image', are given the task of 'filling the land' with their species in order to exercise their special responsibility for life on the land for the Creator Spirit.

God blesses human beings so that they can exercise this function. To 'bless' means to impart life power. By being imparted with this life power, human beings are made partners with God in the task of creating and controlling life on land and sea.

In many translations of the Genesis text, this responsibility for life on the land is called 'ruling' or 'having dominion', an expression which was used to justify the exploitation of the land by European invaders. The parallel creation account in Genesis 2 makes it clear that ultimately the attitude of humans is to be one of service to, rather than exploitation of, the land. The text of Genesis 2:15 (NRSV) reads,

> The LORD God took the man and put him in the garden of Eden to till it and keep it.

Crucial here is the meaning of the Hebrew terms translated 'till' ('abad) and 'keep' (shamar). The Hebrew word 'abad has two meanings, both of which seem to be implied in this text. The first is to till or tend the soil to make it productive. The second is to serve or be a servant to someone. Tending the land, therefore, implies an attitude of respect and service to the land itself.

This attitude of respect extends also to God as the landowner, who has entrusted the land to human beings. It is especially this strong sense of responsibility for the land, entrusted to human beings by the Creator Spirit, that Aboriginal Australians feel so deeply. This deep awareness of responsibility, which has long been present in Aboriginal culture, is clearly the intent of the Genesis text; Aboriginal people knew about serving and caring for the land long before this biblical text was made known to them by European missionaries.

The second verb in this text (Genesis 2:15) is *shamar*. This verb implies keeping, holding and protecting what is given in trust. Human beings are to care for and protect the land which God, the landowner, has given them in trust. For Aboriginal Australians, the specific land entrusted to them is particular areas of Australia. Different clans have responsibility for specific areas.

To emphasise the special role of human beings as agents responsible for the land and life on the land, the Genesis 1 story focuses on the distinctive nature of human beings as creatures in the image of God. The Genesis 2 story, by contrast, emphasises the kinship between human beings and animals.

The story of Genesis 2 again begins with the land as formless and empty (Genesis 2:4b–5). Here the portrait is that of a featureless desert which God transforms into a garden with four rivers (2:8–10).

It is from the very dust of this empty land that God forms the first human. Human beings are made from the land and return to the land (3:19), a belief common to many Aboriginal Australian groups. Although removed from the garden because they did not respect the will of the landowner, human beings are still responsible for the land — even if it is often a difficult task.

Appendix 2

Abraham and the Land: Comments on the Land as Host Country

When the missionaries spoke about the land, they often spoke of the Promised Land of Canaan where God led the chosen people of Israel. They said that Israel had a right to possess that land because God had promised it to the people. And Joshua was hailed as the great hero who conquered the land and so fulfilled God's promise.

But little was said about the indigenous people of the land whom the Israelites conquered. No questions were asked about whether Joshua's scorched earth policy was what God really wanted for the indigenous people. Today Joshua's mode of operation sounds to us very much like that of the British colonial conquerors. Was there another way, a better way? Did the British have to follow Joshua's way?

We believe the story of Abraham offers a better way, a way of peace rather than a way of war. Abraham's way was one of sharing, not destroying. For him the land is a host country, not enemy territory. Abraham respects the peoples of the land and they, in turn, welcome him into their land.

The story begins with Abraham planning to emigrate to Canaan with his father Terah (Genesis 11:31). When they get about halfway, they settle down in Haran. God, however, calls to Abraham and invites him to finish the journey by travelling on to Canaan, where God will bless his household (Genesis 12:1–3).

When Abraham arrives in Canaan there are no problems. The host country seems inviting. The Canaanite people seem to accept him. He travels through the land until he reaches Shechem, where God's presence is revealed. There God is already present as the God of the land (Genesis 12:7). And God promises the land to Abraham.

In the stories that follow, Abraham does not conquer the land and kill the indigenous peoples. Rather, he lives with these people, who willingly share their land with him. Abraham's way is one of peaceful coexistence.

This peaceful way is well illustrated in the story of Genesis 14. Five kings invade Canaan and defeat many of the inhabitants in battle. They also conquer the kings of Sodom and Gomorrah, taking captive some of their people (including the family of Lot, Abraham's nephew) and many of their possessions. Abraham gathers together a small band of 318 men and pursues the foreign kings. By attacking at night he is able to rescue Lot, his family and the possessions of the king of Sodom.

When Abraham returns, the kings of Sodom and Salem roll out the red carpet to welcome him. They enjoy a meal together as a mark of their friendship. The king of Salem is Melchizedek. He is also the priest of the indigenous deity of Salem called 'El Elyon, Maker of Heaven and Earth'. Melchizedek bestows on Abraham the blessing of El Elyon; Abraham, in turn, pays him a tenth of his possessions. (The name 'El Elyon' is translated in the New Revised Standard Version as 'God Most High'. The Hebrew original is an ancient name.)

Then Abraham swears an oath by the God, El Elyon, that he will not take one possession belonging to the king of Sodom. In other words, Abraham recognised the God of the land as his own God, the one who called him to Canaan. In addition, he made it clear that he would share the land with the indigenous people and would not take advantage of any of them. Abraham was a peacemaker, not a greedy invader.

In another story, when a dispute arises over a well that Abimelech's servants have seized, Abraham again finds a way to make peace (Genesis 21:22–34). He even makes a covenant with Abimelech, a Philistine, which ensures that Abraham can settle as a resident immigrant in Philistine lands. In this covenant Abraham again swears by the local deity, El Olam. Again Abraham recognises this God as his own God.

When Sarah dies, Abraham does not just grab a piece of land to bury her. Instead, he follows the accepted legal procedures of the Hittites in the territory and formally purchases a plot, where Sarah is buried (Genesis 23). In so doing, Abraham respects the Hittites, who are called the people of the land (verse 7), and honours their laws.

God makes a covenant with Abraham, promising him that one day his descendants will possess Canaan as their own land (Genesis 15). Does that mean conquest? No! If the way of Abraham is indeed 'the way of the Lord' (18:19), then it is a way of justice and peace, a way of sharing and respect for the God of the land. Abraham's way affirms rather than rejects the indigenous people of the land.

We believe that the Abraham story, rather than the Joshua story, ought to be the model for how indigenous and immigrant peoples are to live in this land. Abraham, the peacemaker, respected the peoples of the land and their laws. We ask the same. Abraham recognised the God of the land. We ask the same. Abraham and the peoples of the land shared mutual blessings. We ask the same.

(For a detailed analysis of Abraham and the land, see Norman Habel, *The Land is Mine: Six Biblical Land Ideologies* (Minneapolis: Fortress, 1995), chapter 7.)

APPENDIX 3

THE BEGINNING AND THE RAINBOW SPIRIT: COMMENTS ON JOHN 1

Our missionaries were good people, but they did not always realise how much the Christian message they presented was wrapped up in a European parcel. Christ was presented to us in such a way that we could not really get to know him. Our missionaries did not acknowledge that the Gospel writers and missionaries in the New Testament, such as John and Paul, were keen to present Christ in a way that was appropriate to the culture of the people to whom they were speaking.

In the New Testament church, we read that some people wanted non-Jewish people to become Jewish before they could become Christians. They wanted them to become circumcised and keep the Jewish law.

But the early church ultimately decided that Christ set people free from these Jewish cultural trappings (Acts 15). The Gospel made people free to be themselves and worship Christ in the terms of their own culture. We Aboriginal Christians claim this same freedom in Christ. We do not have to become European before we can become Christian.

John, the writer of the fourth Gospel, reflects the same freedom in Christ. He is writing for a Gentile Greek-speaking audience. He wants the people to whom he is writing to see that Jesus also belongs to them and is not a foreigner. He speaks to them in the familiar terms of their own culture.

He announces that Christ was with God, the Creator Spirit, from the very beginning. He speaks of this Christ, not in the Jewish terms of a Messiah, but in Greek terms as the *logos*. He commences his Gospel with the powerful words: 'In the beginning was the *logos*' (John 1:1). The usual translation for *logos* is 'Word'.

The concept of the *logos* came from Greek philosophy and referred to a governing principle which ordered the universe or to an immanent power which ordered all things. In John's Gospel, as in the writings of the Jewish philosopher Philo, that power is the agent used by God to create the world and give life and order to all things. God creates the world through 'the Word'. In the Christian Church, the Word is identified as Christ, the Son of God and the second person of the Trinity.

The first verses of John's Gospel read:

> In the beginning was the Word (*logos*), and the Word (*logos*) was with God, and the Word (*logos*) was God. He was in the beginning with God. All things came into being through him, and without him not one thing came into being. What has come into being in him was life, and the life was the light of all people. (John 1.1–4, NRSV)

If we follow the lead of John and consider Aboriginal culture rather than Greek culture, how can we best understand the mystery John portrays here?

For Aboriginal people, the beginning is associated with the life-giving power of the Creator Spirit. This life-giving power is known to us especially through the

Rainbow Spirit. This spirit was manifest as the Rainbow Snake emerged from this land, filled it with life and transformed it into the ordered landscape with which we are linked spiritually. For us, the Rainbow Spirit is Life.

Accordingly, John's Gospel would make sense to us if we paraphrased the first verses as follows:

> In the beginning was the Rainbow Spirit, deep in the land. And the Rainbow Spirit was with God, the Creator Spirit, and the Rainbow Spirit was God. The Rainbow Spirit was in the beginning with God. The Rainbow Spirit emerged from the land, transformed the land and brought all things into being on the land. With the Rainbow Spirit came life, and the life is the light of all people.

Some of us would speak of this power-filled beginning as the Dreaming. (See the note at the end of chapter 1.) Some would prefer to say, 'In the beginning was the Creator Spirit'. And some would see the ancestors as creative powers active with the Rainbow Spirit in the Dreaming. But all of us see the need to recognise that logos is a Greek term which does not readily translate into our culture. For us, the beginning can best be understood in terms of the Creator Spirit we know.

According to John, the *logos* was life and the life was the light of human beings (John 1:4). We too know how life and light have come to our people through the ancestors in the beginning, and especially through the Rainbow Spirit. From them we received our spirits, our stories, our ceremonies and our law. From them we received life.

Ultimately, the Creator Spirit is a hidden mystery, too great for our human minds to grasp. Yet, like many other peoples, our people had a great sense of awe at the incredible mystery we call life. We have long celebrated that life as we have re-lived the creative acts of the ancestors and the Rainbow Spirit in our songs, stories and ceremonies.

The following diagram is designed to illustrate something of the mystery of the life-giving power of the Creator Spirit and its correlation with Greek and Hebrew cultures.

A key verse for Christians is John 1:14, which reads:
> The Word (*logos*) became flesh and tabernacled among us, and we beheld his glory, the glory as of the Father's only Son, full of grace and truth.

The statement that the logos could become a human being and camp among people would have been a bold and staggering new thought to John's audience. But that is precisely what God did in Jesus Christ.

It is just as bold and staggering for Christians to say that the Rainbow Spirit became flesh and camped among us. But that is what the Creator Spirit did in Jesus Christ.

What the Creator Spirit was doing in Jesus Christ was becoming fully one of us. The Creator Spirit hunts with us, shares our food, camps with us, speaks our languages, dances our ceremonies and sleeps by our fires. This Christ is not a foreigner but an Aboriginal person like us. The Creator Spirit belongs to our country. For us, Christ is not European but one of our own, from our land, and present wherever our people are struggling, sick or suffering.

John's Gospel, therefore, helps us to realise that the Rainbow Spirit is not something terrifying or alien, but a power that was and is alive in Christ Jesus. Through Christ, we come to understand an ever deeper meaning to the work of the Creator Spirit. With Christ, we are called to explore the mystery of the Rainbow Spirit which is revealed fully to us in Christ.

APPENDIX 4

THE LAND IN TRAVAIL, AND RENEWED: COMMENTS ON ROMANS 8

Because of our cultural background and historical experiences, certain Bible passages mean a great deal to us. One such passage is Romans 8, especially verses 19–23. This speaks of the whole of creation groaning in travail, suffering with the people, awaiting the freedom which God brings.

Paul here speaks of the whole creation in agony and eagerly longing for salvation. In the past, many missionaries have spoken as if God is only interested in certain individuals, to pluck them out of the world. They tried to teach us that God is not interested in this world, but only in some other spiritual realm elsewhere. Aboriginal people always found this hard to believe. We always knew that individuals cannot be separated from the social group of which they are a part. And people cannot be separated from the land and nature in which they live. Many of our ceremonies celebrate the joy and mystery of life and the inter-connectedness of all things. We see God at work all around us, giving life to the land, animals, plants and people. How can God not be interested in this world? It is God's world. God created it and the signs of God's presence are all around us.

The whole creation belongs to God, not just certain individuals, not just some racial or cultural groups, not just humanity, but the whole creation — social, physical and spiritual!

Paul tells us that the creation is groaning in travail. We know only too well the suffering of our people since the invasion of Australia. But the land also suffers. Our forefathers had laws and ceremonies about caring for the land. They knew that land is sacred and that people belong to the land.

The Europeans did not know the law and the ceremonies of the land. They brought in many plants and animals from Europe and elsewhere which hurt and destroyed God's wonderful creation here in Australia. They brought in farming methods from Europe which also destroyed God's creation. We see white people killing the land and plants and animals with bulldozers, bushfires, erosion and sometimes killing for no reason — they do not even eat what they kill. Our spirits groan — and the land groans, too.

Our people were appointed custodians and caretakers by the Creator Spirit, but in many places we cannot carry out our responsibilities any more. Others have taken over control without knowing the law of the land. We groan because the land suffers and the land groans because we suffer. Our people are exploited because of the greed and ignorance of others. The land is also exploited because of their greed and ignorance. The people and the land are victims of sin.

The narrow theologies which restrict God's interest and salvation to individual humans do not help us. But Paul in chapter 8 of Romans helps us to see that we, as well as the land, are under the bondage of sin and suffering. Paul also affirms that the land aches for salvation and freedom, just as we do. We see Christ suffering in our people who have been separated from their land, who are paupers on the fringes of Australian society, and whose spirits continue to be crushed through the taunts and stereotypes of others. And we also see Christ suffering in the land, which is hurting and damaged as we are.

Paul helps us to theologise our personal experience of exploitation and pain, as well as the exploitation and pain of the land.

But then Paul goes further. He sees the pain as the birth-pangs of a new beginning. Christ not only suffered; he also rose victorious over pain and evil and death. God's love and renewal comes to us in the midst of our suffering and the suffering of the land, and then brings the whole creation to a new liberation in Christ. As Paul puts it: 'The creation itself will be set free from its bondage to decay and will obtain the freedom of the glory of the children of God' (8:21). The whole creation: people, animals, trees, the land and the seas, the spiritual realm — all will experience a new birth.

We who have the Spirit of Christ know this to be true, because we already experience a measure of that new birth, our new creation here and now (8:23). The whole of Paul's chapter affirms this new creation. There is no condemnation for those who are in Christ (8:1). The Spirit of Life sets us free (8:2). The Spirit gives life and peace (8:6). We have hope (8:24)!

For us, the Spirit of Life is the Rainbow Spirit revealed in Christ and now rising again in Christ to free the land from its bondage. For us, the Rainbow Spirit, who has suffered in Christ, is now rising again to free our people.

And so we look forward to the time when once again we will be able to cooperate with the Creator-Spirit to be custodians of the land. With God, we long for the time when the land is once again properly cared for and is fruitful. Its bondage will be over and the land, too, will rejoice with us and worship the Creator Spirit!

Even though we have been dispossessed of our lands, even though our life-giving spiritual tradition has been dismissed as idle fairy tales, even though our supportive extended family structure has been denigrated as primitive, even though our spirits have been crushed as we have internalised what others have said about us, we can still stand confident and bold and declare with Paul: 'If God is for us, who can be against us?' (8:31).

> For I am convinced that neither death, nor life,
> nor angels, nor rulers, nor things present, nor
> things to come . . . nor anything else in all
> creation will be able to separate us from the love
> of God in Christ Jesus our Lord. (Romans
> 8:38–39, NRSV)

Come, Lord Jesus, and renew your whole creation! Come, Rainbow Spirit, and rise again from our land and free it from bondage.

Appendix 5

Profiles of Aboriginal Participants in Crystal Creek Workshops, November 1994 and November 1995

George Rosendale

I'm from Hope Vale from around Cooktown, fifty kilometres north-west of Cooktown. My tribe is Guugu Yimithirr and my grandmother is a Yalandji. I was born at Cape Bedford and educated at Woorabinda. My language, Guugu Yimithirr, is very important for me — it gives value to my life, shows me the importance of who I am. Also, it gives me pride, and direction for my life. For nearly thirty years I've been in ministry. One of the great highlights of my life was at the Bicentenary — I was one of the preachers at this festival. One of the other highlights is rediscovering my Aboriginal theology. It's a great joy for me to sit here and talk about it; I hope that Rainbow Spirit Theology will be something that I have contributed to the whole of Australia.

Nola J. Archie

I come from Mt Isa. My father's people are Garrawa, from MacArthur River; my mother is Waanyii, from Rocklands Station. I was born in Camooweal, Queensland. I minister to my Aboriginal people in the Catholic church in Mount Isa. There are five of us who are elders in the church — we were made elders on Aboriginal Sunday, at the end of Aboriginal Week. We try to make the Catholic church's ceremonies more meaningful to Aboriginal people, especially baptisms and funerals. I think Rainbow Spirit Theology is really great; there's a lot of learning still — a lot of learning from each other, about our Aboriginal traditions, customs, stories, beliefs.

DENNIS COROWA

I was born at Murwillumbah in New South Wales. I have spent most of my life in Mackay, Queensland. In 1989 I was called to ministry among Aboriginal and Islander people in Townsville. My mother and father have given me a mixed family background: Aboriginal, Pacific Islander, Indian, African and European. My wife comes from a mixed background as well. We both share these riches in our family heritage with our children. My experience of growing up as a black person in predominantly white townships, schools and also the churches we attended stirred deeper interest in me about my own cultural identity. Aboriginal and Islander people retaining their culture in any shape or form was always discouraged; little was passed on to us. I was ordained in the Uniting Church in 1994. This workshop has contributed greatly to my understanding of the revelations through native people — the footprints in our history of God's work in creation.

WILLIAM COOLBURRA

I was born on Palm Island in 1945. I wasn't born in the hospital — I was born in the bush. My mother and my father are from the Cape York area. My mother is Olkola and my father is Kuku Jawa. Up Laura way, they call them the Taipan people: my totem is the taipan. I grew up at Palm Island and was educated in the State school system and I went up to the eighth grade. I spent sixteen years in the army. In August 1966, at Lon Tanh, I made a promise to the Lord that if I survived that battle I would give my heart to the Lord. Coming back to the Lord was a slow process for me: I tried to crawl to the Lord instead of walk. We came here to Crystal Creek, not only for ourselves but for all Aboriginal people — so that we can come to the Lord in the way that we can understand him. And I know that the Lord has been with the Aboriginal people since the beginning, that God is speaking to us in what we do and in what we say.

EDDIE LAW

My name is Eddie Law. I come from a small town called Eidsvold. My tribe is the Koreng Koreng tribe. I became a Christian in 1981. I went to do my training at Nungalinya College in Darwin. When I found that their teaching was also teaching in our cultural ways, I started to really identify with my old people: they became alive within me because through the stories that they told me I could see the Gospel really clearly. This Rainbow Spirit Theology is also about growth for our people, Christian growth, developing our own, what we own as Aboriginal Christians.

JAMES LEFTWICH

I was born in Cairns in north Queensland, although my mother was born at Yarrabah mission. My grandmother came from the Kuku Yalandji tribal area around Black Mountain, Rossville, south of Cooktown. My grandfather came from Fraser Island — he was of the Butulah tribe on Fraser Island. They were both taken to Yarrabah as young people. My father is a black American; he wanted my mother to take me and my brother to America to live with him there, but my grandparents, my mum's parents, wouldn't let her go. One of the greatest things in my life was meeting my wife, who was largely responsible for me coming back to the church. In 1987 I was deaconed and then in 1988 — twelve months later — I was priested. I'm now the director of the Aboriginal and Islander ministry in Cairns.

JASMINE COROWA

My parents both have South Sea Islander and Aboriginal ancestry; my father also has some African, and my mother has some Welsh ancestry. I first became involved with art while at high school — not Aboriginal art but European art. I did a two-year Associate Diploma in Aboriginal and Torres Strait Islander art at TAFE. Now I am right into dot painting! I learned a lot about my Aboriginal background through the TAFE course; I would still like to learn more about my Aboriginal and South Sea Islander heritage. I am proud to be an Aboriginal person and artist; I am glad to be able to demonstrate that I am an Aboriginal Christian through my work. In the future, I would also like to work on bark with traditional materials. Working as an Aboriginal artist has taught me more about my own background, and helped me become more involved with the Aboriginal community in Townsville.

6 Bibliography

Dodson, Patrick (1973), *This Land Our Mother*. CCJP Occasional Paper, No. 9. Melbourne: Collins Dove.

Gondarra, Djiniyini (1986), *Let My People Go. Series of Reflections on Aboriginal Theology*. Darwin: Bethel Presbytery.

Gondarra, Djiniyini (1988), *Father You Gave Us the Dreaming*. Darwin: Bethel Presbytery.

Habel, Norman (1995), *The Land is Mine: Six Biblical Land Ideologies*. Minneapolis: Fortress.

Reynolds, Henry (1989), *Dispossession*. Sydney: Allen and Unwin.

Rosendale, George (1993), *Spirituality for Aboriginal Christians*. Darwin: Nungalinya College.

Rosendale, George (1988), 'Aboriginal Myths and Customs: Matrix for Gospel Preaching', *Lutheran Theological Journal* 22, pp. 117–122.

7 Acknowledgements

The authors and publisher wish to thank and acknowledge the following for the use of copyright material: Henry Reynolds, *Dispossession*, Allen & Unwin, Sydney, 1989; George Rosendale, *Spirituality for Aboriginal Christians*, Nungalina College, Darwin, 1993; Djiniyini Gondarra, *Let My People Go*, Bethel Presbytery Northern Synod of the Uniting Church, Darwin